DISCOURSE TO YOUNG LADIES.

SERMON

BY

REV. BYRON SUNDERLAND,

PASTOR OF FIRST PRESBYTERIAN CHURCH, FOUR-AND-A-HALF STREET

DELIVERED THE 22D DAY OF JANUARY, 1857.

WASHINGTON:
CORNELIUS WENDELL, PRINTER.
1857.

WASHINGTON, *February* 27, 1857.

REV. AND DEAR SIR: The undersigned concur in the opinion expressed by many, (and so far as we know without a dissenting voice,) that the sermon you delivered on Sabbath evening last, addressed to "*females,*" should be printed for the benefit of your audience, and for more general circulation.

You laid the public under weighty obligations to you for the sound views entertained, and for the ability displayed in presenting them.

In behalf of others, and for ourselves, we ask for a copy of the discourse for publication.

Most sincerely yours,

ELISHA WHITTLESEY,
SAMUEL GALLOWAY,
WILL. CUMBACK,
WM. H. CAMPBELL.

Rev. BYRON SUNDERLAND.

WASHINGTON, *March* 2, 1857.

GENTLEMEN: The discourse is at your disposal, but I ought to have the benefit of the consideration that I had no thought of its publication, and have now no time to revise it.

Very truly,

B. SUNDERLAND.

To Messrs. E. WHITLESEY,
S. GALLOWAY,
W. CUMBACK, and
W. H. CAMPBELL.

DISCOURSE TO YOUNG LADIES.

"FAVOR IS DECEITFUL AND BEAUTY IS VAIN; BUT A WOMAN THAT FEARETH THE LORD, SHE SHALL BE PRAISED."—Prov. 31, 30.

In assuming to address you of the other sex, I feel some hesitation, because I lack in my own nature a woman's heart. It is not for one who cannot know from his own experience your peculiar emotions and sentiments, under all varieties of circumstances, to tell you the best things for your mission and your time. It needs that heart should speak to heart, and soul to soul. You must have a thousand suggestions of which we of the other sex are wholly ignorant. It takes a like nature thoroughly to comprehend its like. Then I see that this grosser, ruder man's nature of mine, that comes forth out of the dust, cannot fully divine that gentler, rarer nature of yours, which did not so directly spring from the earth. Nor, perhaps, can I speak to you so very well or wisely of the influence of outward circumstances and conditions upon that more instinctive, more enduring nature, as when by birth, by education, by association, by fortune, by society, by rank, by station, by your own thoughts and feelings, purposes and desires, your character, example, influence, and action are all touched, swayed, controlled, and fixed in a thousand ways unknown to us.

But then I can come as your brother, standing outside the tabernacle, and say some things to the spirit dwelling within. I may not know how to answer to all the questionings of that spirit, but if I can speak one word only that shall confirm the soul, and be a theme of memory and a source of profit, I shall be thrice repaid.

In the selection of my text on this occasion, I propose to consider the *perils* and the *glory* of a woman's life. Such an antithesis is surely presented in the passage before us; and the subject-matter affecting you in all your relations here, as well as in your final destiny hereafter, may well claim our attention. In disclosing the contrast presented in the text, I suppose the proverb is simply distinguishing between what is merely perishable and passing away on the one hand, and what is imperishable and abiding on the other. As all material comeliness and grace are appointed to change and disappear, so that which is spiritual and God-like shall endure forever; and since we are immortal, we may not always depend on the present forms of physical loveliness which we see around us; for if, trusting in them alone, a time shall come when they are found vanishing like shadows, then truly must we begin to realize the folly of embarking all our highest interests, and all our essential happiness, on elements so mutable and inadequate for support. It is in this sense that "favor is deceitful and beauty is vain"—not that a moral obliquity is intrinsic to anything of real sweetness, elegance, or splendor, especially that of the human form, and more especially that of woman. The term favor, here used, literally imports *a handsome person*, and metaphorically the partiality and attention attracted by it; and when this is said to be "deceitful," a reference is had to the over-estimate likely to be made of its comparative value and changing nature; and when that beauty which comprises the blandishments and fascinations of the human presence is said, as here it is, to be vain, the significance evidently must be that these personal charms, however striking or glorious they may be for a time, must at length give way before the remorseless progress of advancing age; and then, while sorrow, and care, and change, plough their great furrows over the whole being, we begin to find that what once so excited and entranced us, no longer remains behind.

But then, on the other hand, there is a thing in the female character which constitutes the noblest ground of praise, and that thing is "the fear of the Lord." This is the Old Testament expression for genuine piety of heart and life. *God* and *the world* are terms which tell of the two great devotions of the human race. He that fears God cannot be of this world. He that follows the world cannot serve God. There is a high sense in which these propositions are certainly true; and now, as the dominion of the *material* prevails over that of the *spiritual*, and as all our deepest dangers spring from this condition, so we may consider that in the broader sense of the proverb we are forewarned of all those perils which are especially incident to the sex, and that, in the assurance that "favor is deceitful and beauty is vain," we have an intimation of those subjects which are likely to endanger, either directly or remotely, a woman's character and influence, and final happiness. And yet, on the other hand, we are plainly told in what her true glory lies; and the proverb, in pointing us to "a woman that fears the Lord," and in declaring that such a one "shall be praised," affirms in fact not only a great truth, but a great hope, and most befitting honor and blessedness, as a possible inheritance for all the daughters of the human race.

Before proceeding, however, to point out the *perils* or to explain the *glory* of woman, as derived from the exposition I have given of the proverb, let me remark, by way of caution against mistake, that all beauty, whether it be of matter or mind, of body or soul, is in its gradations, and relative rank and worth, as the creation of God, by no means to be reprehended. The sense of our own nature hails and blesses it unceasingly—spontaneous admiration rises from the human spirit whenever brought into its presence—and there is no need to deny a fact which flames so brightly throughout the universe. Nay, shall we not say that God, our Heavenly Father himself, has an infinite love of beauty? Wherefore has he scattered it in such variety and profusion through all his works? Wherefore has he made all things comely in their place? Wherefore should it teem together in the whole temple of the creation, as though the divine Lord had poured out the exuberance of his own exhaustless spirit? Nay; who shall not feel exhilaration amid the wonders of the universe as he goes forth into its glory, and beholds the handiwork of the Deity, all touched and garnished with the most delicate as well as the most sublime traceries of the infinite and immortal God! Fragments only may we see of the stupendous fabric; but in the compass of that horizon which bounds our finite vision, there is nothing to our apprehension so fair and so exquisite, whether of the material or the spiritual, as female loveliness. It is the rarest earthly type of all the divine creations. Strange that in striking the universal sense of admiration, it should kindle at once so many passionate and unholy fires; and strange that such a gift, lavished in so many gradations, should become a source of peril, both to those who possess it and those who behold it.

But it is not simply in the charms of her person that woman is to be regarded. When we think of the influence of the sex upon the fortunes of the world, in keeping full the tide of successive generations, in moulding human society, and in giving drift and direction to the affairs of men; when we see that, notwithstanding the supreme delicacy of her nature, the comparative sequestration of her life, and the retiring modesty and unostentatious sphere of her activities, she does hold a powerful and unextinguishable dominion over human customs and laws, over the temper and tone of civilization, the policy of nations, and the very constitutions of states and empires; and when we see that she has actually turned at her will in different periods the great currents of the history of the world, and has left her impress on the ages, the fruits of her doings in all the great epochs and stirring events known in the records of mankind, we begin to feel that she must be the subject of a most solemn individual and personal responsibility; and that it is of exceeding consequence that a being who is to sway this peculiar and controlling power, should be herself informed by some high and sacred and unwavering principle, fitted to her nature and condition, and which she herself, and all men, ought to count in her above the price of rubies; because, most clearly you of the other sex, holding such a part in the economy of human life, must of necessity in a world like this be liable to peculiar dangers, and by the same necessity should require for yourselves some adequate security against them. We all live in the midst of perils. It seems coincident with our very existence. Whatever tends to distract or divert us from the high and spiritual aims which God has appointed for our legitimate and proper destiny, is a source of danger. All our exposures to influences that would harm the soul, or drag it down to the pursuit of perishing and unworthy objects, are but so many conditions of trial in which there is imminent jeopardy. And it is to the notice of some of these exposures of your sex that I would now call your attention.

1. First of all, and as that *specific* which is made in the text to stand for the entire sum of your earthly hazards, I mention the exposures of woman from the very circumstance of her personal charms and attractions. I will not dwell on this feature of the subject, for your own good sense must suggest the evils which are incident thereto—pride and vanity from within, envy and mischief from without; and I say, let our young girls be forever prevented from attaining the character and reputation of what is known in the gay world as a *fashionable belle.* The life of such a woman is alternate flattery and wretchedness. The path which begun among flowers, will end in desolation and darkness. If you have personal beauty, hold it as a perilous gift from Heaven; not as your pride, but as your discipline; you will find that you will have trouble enough with it before it fades into the sere and yellow leaf.

2. In connexion with this, I mention another set of exposures from the empire of fashion. Extravagance of ornament and apparel is the ruin of many a fortune, and the women of our times are plunging into every excess of expenditure, aping the feudal and monarchic styles. It would take "the wealth of Ormus and of Ind" to sustain the wardrobes and cosmetics of some of our fashionable ladies in the large towns for any length of time; and many a financial revulsion proceeds from this source, which carries down whole families, with aching hearts, from affluence to sudden penury. I believe in neatness, taste, and elegance of dress; but let every woman stop there. It is intemperance to load her person with the substance of an exchequer, and go swimming through the crowd with superfluities enough about her to feed an army of starving beggars for one whole month. If you have wealth, remember its perils;

and, beyond the dictates of a pure taste and genuine refinement, do not suffer yourselves to be tempted ; you may thus prevent a thousand evils which break forth on the community with earthquake violence, and arrest that tide of luxuriance which casts up a thousand shipwrecks along the shore. You alone can cure the crying evils of these times, and your fathers, husbands, and brothers, as well as thousands of the poor who feel this plague of extravagance in the higher circles in more ways than one, will bless you for it. Let your adorning be, most of all, the gentleness of a meek and quiet spirit, a woman's exquisite sense of fitness and tender love of soul, conforming the outward appointments in all sweetness and genuine naturalness to the innate love of her diviner spirit. Let the young ladies be not forever vexing parents on the subject of ornamental dress. Make yourselves as beautiful as you may, but do not think of appropriating the enormous sums which are annually wasted to accomplish it. Fall back on your own genius, and supply by your wits the costly materials of foreign climes. It is plain enough that a young girl with her head full only of bodices and robes, and the splendid regalia of a carnival of pleasure, will be in a little while so utterly intoxicated with those fairy visions of evanescent excitement, as to apprehend nothing whatever of a more sober or substantial nature ; and the maiden that goes forth under the spell of such a dilirium may float, indeed, for a few brief hours, like Cleopatra when she came to meet Antony, but she may also come to feel the aspic's sting, and die like her a death of shame and violence. Let those who put their trust in things no more abiding beware of the fatal consequence.

3. Another exposure of woman is to the dangers of a false, defective, or mistaken education. There are many

parents who are more to be blamed than their children; and if the children need correction, the father and mother need it more. It is amazing how the bands of family government have been dissolved and weakened; young people have usurped the dominion to an amazing extent. Parents, in doting fondness or criminal indulgence, have permitted them to do so; and now childhood and youth imitate the functions of age, and the old men reduce themselves to the level of boys in their most wild and untoward moods; so that much of the reverence and respect of gray hairs and long experience has passed away. The sex cannot but feel the deleterious influence of this state of things. A daughter thus permitted, petted, and spoiled, without restraint at home, goes where she lists, does what she will, and fills herself with all the broken morsels and brimming cups of social dissipation. Late hours, questionable associations, sleepy mornings, and indolent habits, cross tempers, and appearances of deception, and that peculiar sycophancy of the fashionable coteries, are the consequence. Our girls grow up in love of idleness, small talk, unused brains, untaught fingers, till they become, alas, in too many cases, but the mere puppets and playthings of the fashionable hour, which in its feverish brevity is passing away, to leave them in the disconsolate vacuity and insignificance which follows. I believe in the accomplishments of a generous and substantial education. I believe in the knowledge and acquirements of womanhood, and in the lighter decorations of the noble arts. But I also believe in the thorough homebred experimental acquaintance with every department of frugal and provident housewifery. I believe in the harp and the piano, but full as much in the music of the spindle and the simmering of the kettle. You shall take one of our young ladies, whose education has been restricted to what she attains in our fashionable boarding schools, and that rounded off and completed by the dancing master and the music master, and finally practised to perfection when she comes out into society, and ends in the crowds of the pleasure-seeking, wherever and whenever and whysoever they may be assembled—you shall take such a woman at twenty-five, and put her at the head of an establishment, with the responsibilities of wife and mother resting upon her, and then you will begin to perceive that her whole previous course has only tended to render her now an object of commiseration. If she have the elements of a true woman, she will then begin in vain to regret the loss she has sustained, and often in discouragement seek to repair what she now sees is, alas, but too hopeless and incurable. How different from all this is the exquisite description of one who, from her own native sense and judicious training, stands up in the lot of her appointment an ornament and a blessing. "The heart of her husband doth safely trust in her, so that he shall have no need of spoil; she will do him good and not evil all the days of her life; she seeks the wool and the flax and worketh willingly with her hands; she is like the merchant-ships—she bringeth her food from afar; she stretcheth out her hand to the poor, yea, she reacheth forth her hands to the needy; she is not afraid of the snow, for all her household are clothed with scarlet; she maketh herself coverings of tapestry, her clothing is silk and purple; strength and honor are her clothing, and she shall rejoice in time to come. She openeth her mouth with wisdom, and in her tongue is the law of kindness; she looketh well to the ways of her household, and eateth not the bread of idleness; her children rise up and call her blessed; her husband also, and he praiseth her. Her husband is known in the gates when he sitteth among the elders of the land.'' No woman can realize this picture to herself and her family who has been trained exclusively in the present polite schools of study or of etiquette. We need some of the sterner qualities of our grandmothers—of the women on the stage in the days of the Revolution—who could bake bread and give cheer to a poor soldier on his way to the field of conflict; we need this great heroic element infused into the volatile spirits and giddy natures of this generation, that we may preserve the very foundations of society from decay and dissolution.

4. But another class of exposures incident to the sex arises from solicitations of acquaintance, companionships, and the frivolous and desultory aims and objects constantly presented to their attention. Is it not true that a large portion of the time of ladies is consumed, and their energies distracted from genuine pursuits, in the multiplicity of calls and returns of calls, cards and counter cards, civilities and counter civilities, and ten thousand cold formalities, and the usual quantity of common-place remarks, which, like heaps of rubbish, are thrown in to fill up the interstices of a web of life that would otherwise be so flimsy as scarcely to hold together? And is it not true that each individual member of the whole social circle feels herself beleaguered and overwhelmed by a host of acquaintances who become the very annoyance and vexation of her soul? She dreads the ringing of the door-bell and the announcement of the company. She meets them, however, with a smile of warmest greeting, and inwardly wishes they may soon be gone. It is one of the most pernicious evils of our factitious life; we all feel it, and yet we know not how to remedy or remove it. I pity

the poor damsel who is compelled, from the tyranny of custom, to sit through the tedious hours of a whole evening for the entertainment of some simpering dandy, who vainly imagines he is conferring a distinguished honor by his presence and attention, when perhaps during the whole scene he has not been able to express the ten-thousandth part, or the most minute fraction of the very smallest infinitessimal of the shadow of a single sensible idea. Now, I say the ladies are under no obligation to undergo such intolerable vexation as this, and if they would take it in hand they might, to a great extent, remove or correct it. I would that the whole race of creatures in the shape of men, who can show themselves capable of stealing and worse than wasting a woman's time, might be utterly expunged, and it is your fault if you do not thoroughly route and disperse them. And as it is with persons, so with books. I know not what you read, and if you read with discretion I would not inhibit anything; though to bury one's self in the trashy novels of the day, to the neglect of other and higher pursuits, is indeed unwise. The mind becomes tinged with a false coloring of life, and the whole tone and temper of the soul is rendered romantic and impracticable. I believe, however, there is a worse evil than this prevailing to an alarming extent among classes of the ladies, and that is the not reading at all—the total ignorance of standard works of merit—so that in conversation with one of these a sensible man would soon perceive, however attractive the personal appearance, that he had met with a sheep in a golden fleece. However, I will pass to say—

5. There are perils springing from the accepted and settled amusements of the world to which the sex are imminently exposed. It is into this great maelstrom of what the world

terms polite and fashionable life, that thousands yearly plunge, never to come out again till all is ruined. Now I am not going here to discuss seriatim the comparative or intrinsic merits of these customs or institutions. I know very well the difficulty of this. There is a whole circle of ethical questions that stand like trees in a morass; they totter and shake at every tread, in every blast of the strong wind or the storm, and yet it is difficult to surround or uproot them. But of the general effect of dissipation on the mind and heart there can be no doubt—the feverish excitements, the petty annoyances, the ignoble suspicions, the delusions, the deceits, the heartless parades, the dangers of health in body and mind, and the blinding, barren, bewildering influence of this broad continent of social festivities, amusements, and entertainments, in every form and quality, render it impossible to be inhabited or frequented by a human being without the contraction of some fell spiritual disease. And yet, it may be asked, if religion prohibits all social intercourse, and sets its mark of reprobation on every variety of relaxation? I answer, by no means. It is indispensable to human happiness and goodness that the mind and body should find relief in every rational enjoyment; and it is not for me to say how far or in what way that indulgence within a prescribed circle may be permitted or required. But here is one stern and ineffaceable line of demarcation between the church and the world—whatever goes to give you the stamp of a worldling in the public estimation, that pertains to the forbidden fruit; and if you touch or taste it, you must do it at your own peril. I think it is very well for communities to prescribe their own amusements; they incidental to society and to human nature; and when, are by a wise discrimination, grounded in the most solid principles, and confirmed by the highest and longest experience, the propriety or impropriety of those amusements has been determined, then let the division line stand forth in bold relief, and let every woman say, so far can I go but no farther. The difficulty, however, is that we do not very clearly distinguish the proper line of demarcation, and we do not always observe it even when understood. Enough there are to break down every embrasure, and mingle and confound all things together in one sweeping hurricane of worldly commotion and excitement. . The result is, that little substantial good is accomplished; and she that went forth in search of self-gratification, returns to lament her deep and bitter disappointment. We are proverbially a fast people, and we carry things to such excess that the recoil often comes with a swift and overwhelming retribution. Now the sex have much to do with this deplorable condition of things; and being themselves among the chief sufferers, it is somewhat singular that they should persist in nourishing the scorpions whose stings they so often feel.

6. I observe again, you are in peril from many a sad experience of human life; there are women who know the sorrows of widowhood and orphanage—of loneliness and desertion—of coldness and neglect—of cruelty and scorn—of poverty and unrequited toil. Into the depths of this terrific abyss of human agitation, mutability, and anguish of soul, I do not care to look. It is enough to see a strong man cast down and writhing under the stroke of the catastrophe which felled him. But on the misfortunes and wretchedness of womanhood I do not care to look. I pass it by, shuddering as I think how many gentle hearts lie quivering there, almost desperate—some in the concealed trouble which is their own bitter secret, bearing it still alone as bravely as they may—

some in desperation, ready to abandon all hope of deliverance, and give themselves up to the furies of temptation, infidelity, blasphemy, and all nameless sin. Oh, what is so piteous as a woman's nature thus thrown down—such intuition, such quickness of sense, such trembling and live emotions all through and through the soul—and yet so delicate, and yet so helpless—with beams of beauty in her darkest hour. Oh, my soul! how fearfully are we made! what hazards do we tread upon at every turn—what great sublimities, and what fearful convulsions in all this wondrous swimming world of life, to make one stand in awe while he looks—while working onward, the vast procession of human souls through storm and sunshine wend their way! Surely, in this view we can comprehend the deeper and broader significance of the proverb, "favor is deceitful and beauty is vain," because in the great perils and giant forms of evil which assail you, there is no security for you in any thing this side of heaven. And now, having noted the first part, I will turn to the second—the consideration of the glory of woman.

And my principle to determine this is also in the text—"a woman that feareth the Lord, she shall be praised;" this is her true glory. It is equivalent to saying that the religion of Christianity furnishes the only principle, truth, or impulse to a true, a genuine, and lasting honor. The soul of a woman informed and garnished with this divine production is then in the condition of genuine piety toward God, unfolding and developing one grace after another, in all the years of life, by the wonderful working of a celestial spirit, by all the truth, and in every providence, upon her awakened nature, to mould and fashion it into a perfect likeness of the only Christ and Savior of the world.

A woman, therefore, under the full effect of the fear of the Lord, is in her true glory, and a thing of praise—because then she becomes the highest and fairest type of God's divine and inimitable art. The arts of human genius are all dead in the comparison to this living work of God's own art; we wonder at them, but here, here is a wonder which may transfix the soul. I verily believe the angels themselves are not more beautiful after their kind, than she who has been turned here on earth into all the sweetness and sublimity of the gospel.

"There is nothing on earth," said Martin Luther, "sweeter than the heart of a pious woman." This he said in memory of the woman Ursula, who had given him bread when he was a poor hungry student, singing songs in the street, that he might gather a few pennies to save himself alive.

She is in her glory, because she is a being of superior taste—that peculiar heaven-descended intuition kindled in the soul, which moves not by a gross and irksome system of mechanic rules, but by the innate sense of all high proprieties and fitting things. She shall be a law in herself, of keenest and most unerring judgment, in all questions of casuistry, or doubtful or contingent import.

She is in her true glory, because now filled and radiant with spiritual loveliness, the sublimest grace of all. The sun of righteousness has risen upon her, and her spirit is become more musical than the fabled statue of Memnon.

She is in her true glory, and a thing of praise, because she is at her highest pitch of influence and power, standing in her own time and place, and creating impressions on the souls of others that will return ever more vividly to their dying day. I see the heroines of sacred story, all standing forth in this light, the mothers of prophets and the sisters of kings.

3

Yea, I see the modern heroines of missionary fame, great names of the chief and honorable women in the host of Christ, not less illustrious in their Christian toil. I know their fame is not Zenobia's fame, which faded out when her own Palmyra fell; nor yet Lucretia's; no, nor yet the fame of the Catherines of France, or of some of the less modern queens of England. Her present Majesty, republican as I am, I willingly except, and believe her to be a right good Christian woman. Nor are such ladies as Mrs. Fry and Florence Nightengale to be overlooked, who have rivalled all the Howards of our sterner sex in their gentler but more intrepid benevolence. Nor will I exclude from the Christian glory of the female character such a woman as Esther in the court of Babylon, or of Josephine in the court of Bonaparte—such a woman as Hannah Moore, or Felicia Hemans, or Margaret Fuller—though this last seemed sometimes so lost in the mysteries of her own soul. But these, and a host of others, I have no space to name. What lights in the firmament of time are they; each found her allotted sphere, and shone in it so brilliantly, giving to the world a new and fresher sense of life; as every woman, be her station ever so humble, or her circle ever so limited, may do, when, with a full soul, she cries to God for the vestal fire and the sacred unction. Therefore, I never looked on any one of the gentler sex, just ripening into womanhood, that I did not feel how sadly out of joint her life must be, with no dwelling in her heart of the mighty presence of the Holy Spirit, never yet being kindled with that consummate love which God alone gives by faith in Jesus Christ; for it is that love alone which produces fear—the fear described in the text—the fear of the Lord. It is not a slavish, not a servile fear, but filial fear, that makes this daughter now doubly a daughter of God by renewing grace. What I mean, then, is this—that a woman having such a piety in her soul, the tenderness of love, the firmness of truth, the incorruptible steadfastness of virtue, the sweetness of Christian charity and affability—that is my idea of the fitness of things—that is the fitting gem to the fitting casket. Men, young men and old, being relatively speaking a sort of coarser and ruder nature, do go without the grace of God, and that is bad enough; but when I see a fair young being of the other sex, growing up without the fear of the Lord before her eyes, blushing in all the crimson radiance of her own loveliness, and flourishing in her own endowments and prosperities, and languishing out her brief and fleeting day upon the stage where others before her have so often shone with equal power and brilliancy, yet in forgetfulness of God and all sacred obligations, then I am shocked, absolutely shocked. Why, a woman without Christ, without the sweet filial fear of the Lord who made her in her heart—yea, and without the hope of the cross of Christ—a bright and lovely woman, all in her delicacy, all in her refinements, all in her full accomplishments, to be defective here, in the very vital and substantial force of her noblest life and being—that is really too sad a sight. Ah, indeed, it is hanging sweet garlands of fresh flowers around the tombstones of the dead, and scattering all fragrant perfumes over the rottenness of the grave. I know enough of the woman's heart, unless she be very simple and superficial indeed, to know that there is growing up one great capacity for one great superhuman and unexcepted love; and that nothing short of God in his fatherly compassion, and Christ in his most sweet, melting, brotherly and bride-groom tenderness, can ever satisfy that craving; and I therefore think, when I see her going without the fear of the Lord, how sad the poor child must be, when, after a few months or years of earthly pleasure, she comes down from the heights of gaiety and pride, and sits in the valley of desolation, to feed on the bitterness of disappointment, and find all her pleasant things laid waste forever. She may have depended on the flatteries of admiring crowds around her; she may have snuffed the incense of idle adoration in the vain and giddy round of this world's frivolities, and in this sense has she been praised; but oh! how hollow, how empty, by and by, when sobered she sits down from the intoxication and delirium of those earthly mazes, all gilded with the meretricious smiles of an unnatural, over-heated, and swift-consuming society! All such applause shall seem, by and by, to the soul's returning consciousness, like an expiring moon beam, like shadows, gone forever; and then, then if the woman have indeed a deep woman's nature, what will she do with the hunger of her own soul, or how dispose of those vain regrets? Oh, how give up the images of her own idolatry! A thousand chances are to one, if in her despair she sink not, like Satan falling into the darkest infidelity, into the most abandoned courses of sin and condemnation, and into the deepest depths of hell, both here and hereafter; for a woman's mind moves quicker than ours, and she makes her choice, and gets far out on her way, before we in our stolidity have time to stir. Have you not seen the race run here, especially in the metropolis, of more than one such woman; and have you not witnessed in your own day her premature and miserable end? And where are her flatterers now? Where are those wretched miscreants in human shape that swarmed around her, blazoned and bedecked with all the trappings of highest, gayest, fashionable life? Where are the villains, that smiled and smiled upon her, while she took them for honorable men, and reveled in their honeyed words, and seemed to float in heavenly aroma through all the balmy atmosphere of their attention, praise, and obsequious court? Where are they now? Flown like the summer birds when the cherries blush no more in the boughs, and the rare downy flush begins to blacken on the rotting peach; and now the poor daughter of delusion at length perceives the worth and substance of all that human praise; now she knows how much it will comfort her in her hour of need; now she beholds what furnishing it gives her to meet neglect and cold indifference, obscurity, solitude, sorrow, and desolation. I bethink me of one such—the Countess of Blessington—whose life was more than full of the attentions of all the distinguished, honored, and illustrious men of the world in her own times, writing at last in the bitterness of her soul, and saying—"I look in vain on every side for consolation." Oh, what anguish succeeding to the fevered pleasures of this world. Let me not speak too harshly when I say, a woman is a fool that will thus consent to take up her course through this world without the fear of the Lord before her eyes, and the love of Jesus in her heart, and the immortal hope of the Christian religion beating in the soul, and undertake to tread on through all the great vicissitudes of her career, and all the rigorous changes of her fortunes, and all the nameless suffering, and all the sad catastrophes of her existence, hoping for help from the base and treacherous elements of the factitious society by which she is surrounded.

Now, I say the grounds on which, in reference to final character and experience, we ought to rest the true valuation of her worth and praise, are somewhat like these—contentment with her providential and appointed lot, and patient endurance, heroic fortitude and continuance in well-doing in the same; then some useful, exalted, appropriate aim of life—such an aim as may call out all those untried and unexhausted powers which lie folded in her gentle nature, and which shall adorn herself while they pour blessings upon others—indeed, the one great aim of a Christian woman's virtue, inflamed and kindled by her Savior's love; then a full and practical recognition of her own genuine sphere and acknowledgment of God therein, in those vital relations of daughter and sister, wife and mother; for no true woman informed by the light of God's holy word, and made rich and gentle still more thereby, can go before the world with brazen-faced audacity, and blaspheme God and denounce the state, because she is not created or rendered greater than man in mere authority and power. No, rather you shall find her in a gentle, quiet, but faithful discharge of the duties of her state, and in shedding such a constant influence of reclamation around her, that all who come under the power of her example and her carriage may be the better for it, and go from her with new and nobler views of life—with lighter hearts, and better purposes, and holier reverence for sacred things; and this is what the world needs now. Napoleon had it all but right, when he said France needed mothers; I would add, daughters and wives, and sisters too. Oh, if our women would spend but half the time which they now spend in the vain and evanescent pursuits of fashion and of folly, on those goodly deeds of charity to the poor—on those great sacred movements of Christian beneficence to the world—how soon would Paradise begin to bloom in this wide wilderness of misery and crime. I know the enduring nature of a genuine Christian woman, and I can divine her works, so that playing out this part to the end of life, she may go freighted to her heavenly home, not alone with the best memories of her kindred, but of thousands of others, who when they first knew her were ready to perish, but whom she reclaimed. Yea, and that so living, she may come at last to the heavenly gate, and be welcomed there as already an angel of light, leaving behind her the radiance of her flight to guide the wanderers whither she has gone! Such, I say, are the true grounds of a woman's praise—a praise not fleeting, but to last forever—a praise that she shall wear amid the immortal and uncreated glories of the world of light, nor blush to own it there!

Now, I say, the principle of practical operative faith, such only as the religion of Christ affords, and what is the same thing, she that feareth the Lord, for that was the Old Testament way of stating the matter, is alone competent to make your life, young ladies, what it ought to be for your own sake, for your friends' sake, for the sake of those whom you are to influence through life, and for the sake of those everlasting interests which are vitally bound up in you, and with you, and which your own destiny is sure to carry along with it whatever may be its ultimate direction; and never can a true woman say that the mystery of her own life is really solved, till she comes to feel the great spiritual life of God beating in her own soul; the power of his grace in the Son of God making her own soul's temple its abode, and lending new and rarer charms to the beauty that is already there.

1. I have spoken of contentment in your lot as a ground of praise. Women have a busier ambition than even the other sex, and therefore the mind's agitation is more severe. The ungratified desire must find vent, or else 'twill drive its shaft down deep into the soul, and let forth there its tides of grief.

Thus it is, that we see all manifold humors in the gentle sex—some rush into authorship ; some seek the gay scenes of life; some live in one wild dance of feverish excitement; some betake themselves to the realms of written romance, and spend their sensibilities in the great morass of fiction ; some go to baser purposes, and reach more terrific and abandoned destinations. But the true woman who feareth the Lord, where is she? Treading, all noiselessly but firmly, the path appointed by her Heavenly Father. Hard indeed it may be, but she knows that path must lead to glory, and honor, and immortality. She has no wish to carve out a path of her own, for well she knows it is far better to endure and faint not all the ills which Heaven may appoint, than fly to other ills, created not in mercy, but for the punishment of our disobedience and rebellion against the ways of God. Now, then, look there and see that genuine *Christian* soul, bearing up heroically under every form of trial, guided not by the untamed and erratic impulses of degenerate human nature, but leaving her way to be carved out by Him into whose hands she has committed her soul ; and smiling, in all the storm and darkness which fall around, at the great thought, how little these can do to touch her spirit with essential harm. To her the Bible is become the sweetest bread of life. Before that book, why she may have read novels, and may have enjoyed herself at play-houses, and found some little crude and unripe pleasure among the pastures of this world. But now that she has found the letter of her Father in Heaven to her soul, and sees in its great unsealed pages a mystery more awful and more entrancing than novelist ever wrote, and studies there the insight of human character and life, and spells out a wisdom mightier far than sage or poet ever knew, and takes hold for herself on that amazing and immortal life, of which the present is but a passing prelude ere the curtain is hoisted from eternity's awful front; why, there is no more charm for her in this world's gay scenes; they dissolve, and part, and sink away; they roll down together like the dust; and her feet, all sandalled with salvation, go over them tripping as a fawn.

2. I have spoken of the aim of life as a ground of praise. Now, there are multitudes of the sex who grow up in the ordinary walks of life, and are so conditioned as to feel no doubt that they have really no great aim of life. The whole of the period of childhood and youth is spent in dreams and visions of the future, to which indeed they cannot penetrate, and which often take away the stimulus of exertion; and so they spend all their energies in small, comparatively small, matters—the daily scandal of the town, the small talk, the novels, the fashions, and the nonsense of the day; and thus life yields no great fruit; and many an hour of suffering does a woman know, while thus she feels that she is doing nothing worthy of her own soul. I think, indeed, it is proper for every woman to prepare herself for whatever state may chance for her, and be ready to meet it when it comes; but I know there is only one aim that can fill the soul, and that is the glory of God and the promotion of his kingdom, which again is only fear of the Lord, leading to all right and noble action. And when one can get this uppermost, then there will be a manifestation of activity and zeal in all wonderful directions. And the works of such a woman shall praise her before all men. And here let me say, that those women who become the mere puppets of an idle, simpering, disgusting, and shallow life, gain nothing at last. They cannot, after all, stand in the reckoning of the sober judgment of mankind. They must invari-

ably sink in the estimation of the good not only, but even of the bad; for the time will come when their flatterers will desert them, and the life which began in brightness will go out in clouds. But when the soul has been put on fire with the love of the Savior of the world, and those great thoughts, begotten of the gospel of God's grace, begin to shine forth in a woman's life, then you have set a treasure in the casket worth the having, for you have made the finest and fairest type of human nature to be the conservator of the noblest and grandest faith which ever came out upon the world. And those principles and thoughts shall flame forth and be a light in her utmost darkness, and comfort and sustain the spirit when all else fails. Surely it shall be a glorious triumph, to see the delicate but stricken one walking with God in the midst of the furnace, and being more than the asbestos, unconsumed thereby. It is thus that the two fittest things are seen together. Often it is a subject of sarcasm among the grosser of our grosser sex, that the religion of Jesus is just fit for weaker woman. Yes, but it is the fitness of a glorious sunset over the face of nature in her most glorious moods. No doubt the celestial light beams more radiant on the fair brow of a woman's purity, and falls more gently into her serener soul; because there is a high and sacred fitness in her nature to it. And on this account, as I have before intimated, I have often wondered at those who live in this world without the religion of Jesus. A woman devoid of the sweet spirit and high hope of the gospel, is to me a mystery—the flower without its choicest fragrance, the fruit without its flavor. No such shall live in yonder scroll of fame, the highest heraldry of Heaven's court; they have no life there beyond the temporal and passing scene, and none that shall merit honor, when the present world has disappeared.

3. It is some ground of praise, which only the woman that feareth the Lord can attain most perfectly, to recognise and abide in her own proper sphere of action. In all ages there have been breaches on the law of appointments by unquiet and ambitious spirits—women who rise up in their restlessness, and in deeds of desperation would turn over all existing institutions, and produce one scene of anarchy and confusion. We have such a class in our own land at the present moment—strong-minded women, as they are termed. One sad and melancholy feature of these misguided individuals is, that they are all infidels, or act on the principles of infidelity; with them the Bible is a book of fables, and the whole gospel-way of salvation a ridiculous imposition. They have grown wiser in their own esteem than the word of God; and, casting this light away, they rush out in the darkness of their own unaided reason, making disgrace of the very name of woman, so that all the world laughs after them. Not such, indeed, is she who feareth the Lord. There is a certain intuition whereby she knows her place and keeps it. Certainly I would not restrict the noble impulses of a woman's nature under the influence of the guiding power of Christianity. I know not to what high or lowly mission she may be called—like Deborah of the Old, or like the Dorcas of the New Testament; like the Maid of Orleans, or like the mother of Washington. Far be it from me to say whither your direction lies. It is God-given, and you must seek it at the foot of the throne of grace. It cannot altogether be determined by conventional rules, and yet the true woman lays hold on those great fundamental and established relations of life, and makes them like a new revelation to those around her—daughter and sister, wife and mother—these are enough for her. She teaches how to

live in these, and makes them answer for the whole scope of her activities. Because, while thus in her own orbit she constantly sheds her light afar upon other paths, as when the sweet influence of the Pleiades descend upon our solar system, and silently but majestically waft them through the infinite space toward the one grand central throne—so, out of her sphere, she affects the state and all human institutions, and finally the eternal destiny of the soul itself. Who can tell what one such woman can do to bless her husband and her children, and all men about her? The waves of her influence will roll afar, nor ever cease till they strike on the eternal shore; nor then, so long as ages last. We need to see such a woman in the midst of her activities. A most beautiful picture is drawn of her in this chapter of the sacred proverbs, which I have already given. It is exquisite enough to be recited again and again, and let every woman learn it by heart.

Thus, as well as I might under the circumstances, have I set forth the true glory and the ground of praise belonging to the sex. This is your security and safety against the mighty perils to which you are ever exposed. If it be true, I implore you to accept and abide therein. I have seen a woman, not very comely in personal appearance, yet to me of the sweetest expression of the human face—a woman in nowise endowed with the affluence or luxury of life—a woman, far in the rural districts, passing her quiet life away, gentle in her own little sphere, limited and hemmed in by the assiduities of toil—far away from the noise and pomp, the glitter and parade of populous towns; patient overmuch, for she suffered oft, and died at last in the sober and chill November month; and I saw a snow-flake fall silently on her marble brow as she lay so still in the coffin; and the woman was good ever to me and full of prayer, and she did a noble life of service, and bore her suffering so meekly; yea, and when she came to die, she went so sacredly and full of joy; but she spake a word in my ear before she went, as often she had done before. I knew she had done a great heroic deed, for I never forgot that word, and it brought me at last to the foot of the cross. Oh, blessed be her memory in Christ, and sainted evermore. Pardon me, now, you that have the hearts of women, but it was my mother. It takes but little time or space to do a great heroic deed, such as shall be sublimely heroic. The woman in the little cottage can be truly great—eternity will show how great she is—a widow woman perhaps she is, with a few little children, her only *mingled* care and comfort in this world; but she nurtures them up, bearing things which only a heart deep in sorrow knows or can tell; and by and by the jewels of Cornelia begin to shine; and then is the widow's heart blossomed out in a circle of noble sons—the great fruitage of her life—strong and noble men, who go treading like giants in their strength from fame to fame.

Then, my conclusion is, that it is the great work of womanhood to educate the generations in their beginnings; you have all the control then of the issues of life; God has placed you like guardian spirits at the very fountains of society. The vestals that kept the altar fires in the Roman temple had not a more sacred or watchful office to perform than you have at this very moment. If that fire ever went out, it was supposed to bode some evil to the republic; and the virgin through whose negligence it was permitted paid the forfeit of her life, while the fire thus extinguished could only be rekindled from the rays of the rising sun. I believe in my soul that upon you and your sisters in America, in chief, will rest the perpetuity of our own republic, and the peace and the prosperity of the church of God in this land ; you have it in your power to mould the customs of society, and give laws to nations. If the offices of women have never been wanting in any of the great epochs of the world—if a woman perpetuated the genealogy of the Messiah, and was chosen as the instrument of that great mystery of the divine incarnation—if a woman went last from the crucifixion, and was first to make known the resurrection of the Savior of the world—if a woman preserved in its cradle the great idea of the reformation, when Martin Luther was discussing the necessity of abandoning his studies, and becoming a common miner of Mansfield—if a woman has fitted such a man as Washington to become the father of his country, and by this agency established an empire that in less than a single century has grown up to rival the most powerful kingdoms of the earth—then, what is not in reserve for her in the coming mighty events of the future, if only she prove true to her mission, her people, and her God?

And now, you of the metropolis may well bethink you of the places where you stand, and of the millions of eyes that shall watch your course ; you are as a city set upon a hill, and you may give an example here that shall be felt to the remotest corners of the world. I know to whom I have been speaking, and because I know them so favorably, for their many virtues and influential character—for none can hold hold the ladies of Washington in higher esteem than myself—I invoke your more earnest aid, your more unceasing vigilance, in every noble, Christian and patriotic work. I call upon you to protect the fair form of our most holy religion. I call upon you to correct the evil and the disorders of our social life and manners. I call upon you to purify the springs and fountain-heads of the education of our people. I call upon you to give a new impulse to the humanities and the charities of our wonderful civilization. I call upon you to roll back the dark and bitter tide of vice, and crime, and wretchedness, and desolation, which is breaking out, alas, on every hand. I call upon you to stamp your resistless and remorseless reprobation upon the vulgarity, the profanity, the intemperance, that abounds. I call upon you to kindle and keep alive, as well you can under God, the celestial fires of patriotism, philanthropy, and religion, and to send abroad from this metropolitan centre of the world, that high and hallowed influence, more potent than the ministry of angels from heaven for the reclamation of the nations and the autumn fulless and harvest of the world—the influence of a woman, whose beauty and consummate glory is, that she fears the Lord!

www.ingramcontent.com/pod-product-compliance
Lightning Source LLC
LaVergne TN
LVHW020741120826
845150LV00010B/2296

* 9 7 8 1 4 1 8 1 9 4 2 6 0 *